A BOOK OF PEACE

"Have we not all one father?
Hath not one God created us?"
Malachi 2:10

To my children
Bruno, Oliver, Anne, Christopher, Jose, & Maria

CATHERINE DE VINCK

a book of peace

ALLELUIA PRESS

By the same author:

A Time to Gather, 1967 and 1974
Ikon, 1972 and 1974
A Liturgy, 1972 and 1974
A Passion Play, 1975
A Book of Uncommon Prayers, 1977 and 1978
Readings (John at Patmos & A Book of Hours), 1978
A Book of Eve, LP record with text, 1979
A Garland of Straw, 1980

Copyright, © , Catherine de Vinck, 1985
Published by ALLELUIA PRESS,
Box 103, Allendale, N.J. 07401
Printed by Thomson-Shore, Inc., Dexter, MI
ISBN 0-911726-47-0

Two poems, "Hiroshima, mon amour," and "A Time for
Peace" reprinted by permission, "The Harbor Review,"
University of Massachusetts, Boston, Ma.

Design on cover and title page is an ancient Chinese symbol of long life.

TABLE OF CONTENTS

FOREWORD

These poems were written in urgency and sorrow as a meditation on our present historical situation, a situation so dramatic, so untested that we can reflect upon it only in a hesitant, tentative manner.

When the Bomb opened its parasol of fire over Hiroshima, we entered an entirely new phase of our precarious history. Since that fatal day, the consciousness of our fragile human condition is sharper than ever: life on our blue planet appears as a gossamer web that can be torn without any possibility of mending. Death has acquired in this age a new and sinister connotation: in the context of nuclear warfare, death is no longer the natural conclusion of earthly life, but a final solution which would wipe out the human family and transform the earth into a desert of ice in a winter without end. Like the tiger and the whale, human beings are now an endangered species.

Year after year, the terrifying increase in the number of nuclear weapons brings us closer to the edge of the abyss. We can no longer take it for granted that our children will have a future in which to grow, work and realize their potential. Something has disrupted the familiar pattern, something crazy and dark has invaded our world, a power of destruction such as we have never known.

Even language seems to lose its momentum, its ability to express and frame our experience in meaningful terms. Words are vessels, containers and carriers of ideas; they become empty shells when we are faced with horrors our imagination cannot grasp, with numberless numbers our mind cannot begin to understand. What does it mean, twenty thousand million tons of TNT, which is today the sum of the nuclear arsenal? What does megadeath mean? What does it mean to vaporize millions of people? In the words of Marguerite Duras who wrote the script of that memorable film, "Hiroshima, mon amour," "All one can do is talk about the impossibility of talking about Hiroshima."

These poems were written in the context of what is unspeakable, unbearable: yet, the words are not of despair, but of hope. They move from images of death to images of life, from ashes to bread, from emblems of terror to that most enduring symbol of hope, "that light rising over Bethlehem in the East." It is not too late: there is still time to re-form ourselves, to find a common ground of understanding, to live on this earth, not as perennial enemies, but as brothers and sisters engaged in a common work.

The root of war cannot be found in external random events: it is found in the depths of our fearful, trembling hearts. We are not made for war, for the deeds of war: we are made to care for one another, to nurture, to love. It is time to say "No!" to the dark impulses that seek to destroy the beauty of the natural world, the goodness of human realtionships, the simple joy of children, the promise of a liveable future.

I offer this book as a gift of peace, a small contribution to the theology of hope.

HIROSHIMA, MON AMOUR

*"All one can do is talk about the impossibility
to talk about Hiroshima"* Marguerite Duras

Hiroshima, mon amour
how often I held your name
  a shirt of flame around my shoulders
  a coal pressed burning to my mouth!
How often I walked
  into the temple of your wounds
  with offerings of gauze and oil!
I still eat and drink you
  Hiroshima
— in my plate, your white ashes
— in my cup metallic flakes
  iron particles hot to the touch.

I have journeyed underground
  in the silence of bones
  to a place where dry skulls
  flash signals, kindle memories
and my tears, of hard clear glass
have rolled through dark passages
  where children forever sleep
  wrapped in quilts of fire.

Sometimes I think of you
  Hiroshima
as a young woman, alone
  in a center of time, of space
— red silken threads streaming
  from her hands and feet
her voice crying in the wilderness
her words rising like smoke —
  but no one hears
  no one understands
the oracles she speaks.

CHILDREN IN THE LIVING ROOM

Slowly
    lifted by pulleys and ropes
the curtain goes up:
    printed with suns and moons
the cloth gathers in heavy folds.
On the stage
    seated on delicate chairs
children wait for their future.

Papa and Mama have gone out;
they wander through the streets
    shopping for good answers;
in little carts, they heap
    pastel-colored candy dreams;
surely the children will
take and eat the sugar-canes:
    soothing lies, illusions
the words will stick to the teeth
    promoting decay, destruction.

Enthroned in tasselled chairs
    the children wait:
how quiet they are
how smoothly their porcelain heads
    shine in the gilded light!
The smile painted on their faces
    betrays neither anguish nor pain.
But hidden beneath the rigid mask
their real eyes weep: they have seen
    images of exploding machines
    the fragments hurled at high speed
    entering targets of soft flesh.
In absolute silence
    they rehearse the final act:
how death comes crashing
through the door: a power of fire
    a bloody beast
and how flames grow
    out of their shoulderblades
    out of their fingertips
and how they melt
    into droplets of heat
        glistening on the stage floor.

KEEP GOING

"Keep going"
    reads the sign at the corner
but time is running out
    the eviction notice is posted
— the cops are waiting at the door —
"You have one hour to evacuate the planet."

In the mob scene at the movies
    someone never stops shouting
"Keep going! Keep going!"
Drive along the road
    to the lost country
        where houses reappear
        among gardens of roses.
The petals made of dust
    reassemble on long stems
    cup themselves to the sun.
There your mother, your father
    greet you:
you wear ribbons in your hair
    carry a picnic basket
and your heart is a golden locket
    holding faded photographs..

We cannot find the lost story:
the words have been plowed under
    sealed over with concrete and tar.
The place where we were born
    has become a parking lot
and that lovely courtyard
    with its lily pool and carp
has been displaced, transported
    to the dark side of the moon.

Yet there is a confluence:
    moment upon moment
    life upon life
    hand upon hand
a desperate attempt to link
to give love, to draw warmth
    from one another.

At a time when all we hear
    is the door being slammed
        squeezing our fingers
        crushing our hopes
we hold each other close:
our luminous bodies
    smooth as polished stones
ward off the deepening night.

    We keep going.

A LEGACY

Never forgotten
        the scent of childhood meadows
        the ecstasy of afternoons
when time's weight
was violets, primroses
        fragrant in the hand.

We give our memories away.
"Here," we say to our children
"take and eat
        the sacrament of our past;
not wisdom, nor counsel
        mined from the mind's deep cave
but petals floating on air
        unsubstantial fragrance
only the joy of being
        of living innocent and free:
a testament of sorts, a legacy
to be found, to be read
        before the siren screams
        before the monstrous flash
burns the silk of the retina.

Take and keep, learn to cherish
        what is transient, yet changeless:
the sweet odor of the planet
        of violets and primroses
        of milk and flesh
and confirm the joy of it
        through another day."

THERE IS NO OTHER TIME

*"Authoritative estimates put the number of existing
warheads at fifty thousand, enough to destroy every city
in the world many times over."*

Warm in our curtained rooms
    haloed by light of fire and lamp
we make up stories
      spinning white threads of words
          round and round ourselves
    until we disappear:
our mind, asleep in its cocoon
dreams of armored giants called
    to guard treasures and children.

No one can reach us
    so deeply are we lost
      in the tales we invent
      in the lives we are living.
Only the mailman comes in
    — an angel in disguise —
dropping letters from places
    where real flesh bleeds
      under bullets and fists.

We never look beneath the floor
    never break the cellar's locks;
we choose to ignore
    what is stored underground:
      not edible roots, not grain
      not heaps of apples
    but canisters of plagues
    clustered cells radiant with death.

We are not being told the truth
    only soothed with answers
      that will never fit the slot of our fears;
    only lulled into thick layers of lies
      until our voice falls to a whisper
      until language becomes a mumble
        without sound or meaning.

There is no other time
    no other place;
it is not possible to go back

to waterwheel and candlelight
to a past of simple sums:
 chickens counted on fingertips
 years on slabs of notched stone.
Here and now
the deadly spores mulitiply
 grow like mushrooms overnight
  perfecting themselves.
They are harvested
 away from human touch
  in vaults carved in the rock.

In the meantime
 oranges peeled and quartered
ornament the dish
 set before our evening hunger.
We take notice, smile
 admire one another:
how lovely we are, how innocent
 of what is happening outside.
Rivers boil
 cities are crushed like nutmeat
people run in the streets
 screaming;
the heads of prophets rest
 on bloody platters
and from the ancient book of terror
animals appear
 spilled from the pages:
pale horses, dragons
 assorted horned beasts
  announcing the Time of the End.

AGAINST DISASTER

All that was brought over the seas
    tools, sack of grain, seeds
    canvas bags in the hands of mothers
    dolls in the arms of little girls;
all that we carried ashore
    stories, legends, songs
    the words stitched one by one
        carefully by candlelight
    into quilts of many colors
    comforters for the exiled;
all the toiling, all those bodies
    pressed shoulder to shoulder
    to fell trees, to build
        village, town, metropolis:
can all this be erased
    shaken out of the land
        like bitter salt from a box?

We invented a new language
    woven of many foreign strands
        the fabric strong, made to last;
we opened a new space fitted
    to our skill and taste, to our task.
But now the world is all chill and drift;
    plagues ooze from puddles in the streets
    molds grow on cellar walls
    and the poor huddle in doorways
        line up for soup, their lives
        smudged over like small ads
        printed in provincial papers.

What can we shore up against disaster
    against the dread of vanishing
        in the heat of radio-active fires?
We own but our breakable hearts
    our frail paper words cut out
        glued together to form images
        we can prop against the dark:
here, a child's face, smooth
    like a polished precious shell;
there, a water-drop condensed
    into a bit of ragged lace
        we call snowflake:

not much, tokens to mean
    we are conscious, human
    we can still see and touch
    and make small tender gestures
      toward the light.

THE WOOLEN CLOAK

Life as a woolen cloak:
why does this image persist
    when no one now weaves or spins?
I hear the rhythm of the wheel
    the muted sound of the shuttle
        flying from one time-space to the next.
I see the pattern unfold, its texture
    a whispered secret passed
        from age to age, from man to woman
        from mother to child, on and on.
The cloth tears now and then
    burrs are caught in the fleece
        with thorns that prick the hand.
But the work goes on
    its fabric billows in earth waves
        colored according to the weather
            the season:
        silver for ice and moon
        grey for stone and whale
        white for swan and snow
and over all, renewed from year to year
    the polished sheen of leaves and grass.

But suddenly
    for reasons of dissonance
— voices grating against each other
    words shot like bullets
        across boundaries and fences —
the progress of the loom slows down
the wheel comes to a halt
and life, now a thin ragged cloak
hangs by a single gossamer thread
    limp above the void.

MAY DAY

"The world's stockpile of nuclear weapons is now equivalent to sixteen billion tons of TNT. In World War II, three million tons of munitions were expended and between forty million and fifty million people died." The New York Times, October 26, 1982

It is well past Eden:
Adam no longer wears his tribal coat.
The pelt stinking with the dark scent
    of what is wild and free
was left behind at some camping ground.

In the kitchen
Eve turns all things to grace
— It is a good day, a May day:
dough rises on the shelf;
    a lilac branch heavy with bloom
waves, white and bee-full at the window.
She speaks through young lips
each of her words a stitch
    in the ancient quilt of language
tracing stars and rings
    moons honeyed with love.
In the evening she, oh, flows
    wide between the sheets
    a stream he enters.

It is a good day, a May day!
In all places of the world
children smile
    with eyes, hands, limbs.
With their skin they smile
    black and white and yellow smiles
their joy ribboning through the streets
    billowing in the air sailing
        on all the waters of the seven seas.
They say, "Life is good!
    Give us life
        on May day!"

DO WE CARE?

"The way of peace they know not." Isaiah 59:8

We do not know, do not see
do not believe; we cannot move
we have business elsewhere:
the roof leaks, the shoe is lost
there are no candles for the table.
Idle we are not, learning as we do
    how to fold the corners of the sky
    how to twist the fabric of the earth
        into the shape of a napkin
          for trivial daily use.

It is a long time
    since we stopped in our tracks
saw the luminous form of the swan
    as it passed overhead
        carrying messages of air, of water.

It is a long time
    since we looked over the fence
where another geography spreads its maps
    colored with ordinary sights:
        street lamps like our own
        children playing in foreign snows
        old women buying onions
        young ones pleating their hair.

Do we care?
In the book of prophecies
name after name appears
    of cities, districts, towns
    of rivers, bridges, roads
        erased one by one
        as we turn the pages.

Do we care?
Our tinsel glitters
    in the full sun of our ease.
How well creased our pants!
How well buttered our toast!
Our time is money.
Pushed through the slot
the hours give off a silvery sound

as they fall one upon the other.
What do we buy, what do we sell
  to the poor lined up in the streets
    waiting for a cupful of soup?

We have invented ourselves
  in a new world, a place
    where people are numbers on a chart
      pinned on the mind's blank walls.
No face, no voice, no touching hand
no custom, no legend, no village lore
no poetry, neither music nor dance.
And if the luminous swan passes overhead
  bearing the message of wilderness
    of freedom
we can lift the blowgun
and watch as it plummets down
  its feathers snowing on concrete and tar.

Once more, words must be summoned
  must rise from their stony graves
to speak of tenderness, to say
  we are fragile, exposed.
Our skin blisters in the heat
  bruises under blows, bleeds.
Already out future is leaking out
  hour by hour, drop by slow drop
    like myrrh oozing from broken jars.
For our sons, our daughters
  still so close yet so far
    from sundials and waterclocks
will the only certitude be
    death
that silent valet standing
  at their side, holding
    a glass brimful with darkness?

WALKING IN HIROSHIMA

*"The bombs were dropped on Hiroshima and Nagasaki without
warning. A generalized threat had previously been issued to
Japan and thirty-five towns were specifically warned that they
were opened to attack. Hiroshima and Nagasaki, chosen among
other things for their dense population, were not
amongst them."* Blacket, P.M.S. "Military and Political Consequences
of Atomic Energy"

At a safe distance
    on the other side of the map
we sit around the table
    decanting our lives into wine glasses
    drinking to good fortune, to peace.
But the flash on the screen
    opens its corolla: fire rains
    in our minds in hot droplets of fear.
What appears on the lens
    trained on the wrecked landscape:
        tentacles of metal, bone scraps
        a thousand prisms of glass
        catching the slanting light.

At a safe distance
    on the other side of time
we look at the burning town.
They are not real, we say
    these people winged with flames:
only phantoms traveling the air-waves
only shadows painted with red dye.
All is well, we say:
    the day a pinch of sugar
    powdering the tongue;
    the past a fleck of dust
    we blow away at will.

But there is someone at the door:
    hands fumble with the lock
    fingernails scratch the lintel.
Funnelled through almost forty years
    a sound of infinite weeping
    grows louder and louder
    spills into our conciousness:
at last we wake
    enter the nightmare
    inhale the smoke
    count the dead.

A LASTING GESTURE

"Thus says the Lord: I am giving you a choice between life and death." Jeremiah 8:15

To draw order out of chaos
    — a garden, let us say, of edible leaves
    rows of spinach and kale
    where, before our toil
only milkweeds spun their silk—
to build from beams and boards
    wall and roof, a framework
    to hold the compact of life:
such tasks define, confirm
    our name, our place, our skill.

Survival, encoded in the blood
demands of us small gestures.
Why do we store and keep
    the silver tray, the china cup
        we seldom touch or use?
What do we ask
when we slip a golden bracelet
    over our daughter's wrist?
We claim continuity
we beg for remembrance.

The edge is always close:
we fear oblivion, the wilderness
    clawing its way back
    smothering the roses;
roots cracking the pages
    on which we record tone
        texture, inflection
        the fluctuating substance of our soul.

Daily, we go on
    walking, eating, speaking
as if our course were set
    a path straight and endless.
Yet, we know the evidence
and as a last gesture
    of pain, of reckless hope
we fling words into the darkness
    like seeds of light.

SAVE US!

"See for an instant the arc of our vanishing"
Denise Levertov

We follow that curve
    as it descends
        from the neck down to the shoulder
        from the waist to the thigh
        from the space
        — enclosed for us alone
           blue for us alone —
        from sky to land.

We move along such lines
    with eye and wish
    with hope they will endure
        remain sure and true.
But such geometry changes:
    the arc sags
    the flesh wrinkles
    the darkness pools
        where an hour ago there was light.

We are born, we die;
    others pick up the slack.
All right: this too is part
    of the ancient traced pattern.
We take these facts
    pull them over our heads
        like soft familiar garments.
But what if the curve would break
what if life would shrink back
    slippery, boneless
        into primeval shells?
We turn away. Our minds spit out
    the language of extinction:
        nuclear warheads, megadeath.
Good Lord, save us
    do not let us shrug and forget
curled upon ourselves, holding on
    to our toys, our amulets
        our small cache of useless words.
Beyond terror, beyond despair
let us not deny your power
    your peace.

BETHLEHEM

Only twenty centuries
    to count backwards, to reach
        that child born in the straw
while the yellow star of David
    fizzles above the cave
and angels, voices without gender
    sing in the night-sky over Bethlehem.
·Around him,
    the great chain of being whirls
        dances to the light of his eyes
            in time, out of time.

After twenty centuries, discordance
    grating of sounds, of words
        scraped against one another;
language translating itself
    in scribbles on the subway walls
    in a clattering of coins
        spilled on hard counters
        to buy beer or cigarettes.

How long can it stand
    this ancient house
        strong on the ground of our living
when movers wearing helmets and boots
    invade the rooms where children
        in a dancing circle sing:
"Ring around a rosie
    a pocketful of posies
        ashes, ashes, all fall down!"

And they fall down when the old carpet
    is pulled from under their feet.
The fibers worn thin break and ravel.
The delicate oriental pattern
    woven with birds and flowers
tears beyond hope of mending.

For twenty centuries
    he is born over and over again:
The same word, clear spoken
    comes through the burning cloud
    comes through the sealing stone
    comes through the explosion in the air.

His name is Light of Light, Prince of Peace.

AS IF...

"We wait for peace to no avail; for a time of healing but terror comes instead." Jeremiah 8:15

As if a huge needle were at work
lacing together remnants and scraps:
    stories and gestures of love
    the tender moments of life
    bits and pieces gathered
    by patient hands, sewn
        into a good coat
        not fashionable, but warm;
as if there were still hope
    for compassion, for care
and time to find words
    to make up poems, songs, prayers;
as if...

END OF MARCH

Green tones, the silk of words
    unfold from compact buds:
the stems lift themselves
    out of the gummy sticky ooze
raise their amazing substance
    into the air.
It is spring-time. The day fills
    with the sound of new leaves
        new speech: to say what?

It may as well be winter
for the flakes of newsprint
    snow over the land:
grey, dirty, they carry
    the thousand facts caught
        by the camera's blank stare:
a mass of people, refugees
    along a dusty road;
faces behind barbed wires;
life kicked about, bloodied
    limp as a rag doll
        under the boots of terror.

READING THE NEWSPAPER

Beneath the words
    the constant of blood
exposed, darkening the air;
and over and again
    the sound of weeping.

A single theme
    running through
stitching together
    the rags of this world:

war   famine   violence   death.

And my heart flies into pieces
    breaks like a wooden wheel
hitting a rock, at nightfall
    on an old country road.

EASTER

The lie cannot be told
    of a world of simple country lanes
    leading to a peaceful house:
on the table in the breakfast room
    china cups filled with neutral brews.
If you drink it, no taste, no color
    no passion, mistake or risk.

Life happens elsewhere:
see this man laid out in a vault
    his body oiled, packed
        with spices and scented rosins?
He was dragged into dungeons
    thrown into sandpits, pushed
        with cattle-prods into gas chambers:
    he was tortured, beaten, gagged.
No one knew he was that word:
        life
    wedged between sealing stones.

It is happening:
    a language of every day
    a vernacular of delight
breaks through the compact rock.
Pity the people trapped
    in the breakfast room
    with tea and sentimental roses;
pity their mouths rinsed with lies
    their eyes used to the shadows.

See at sunrise this man
    wearing the image of the world
washed clean of death
    and brighter than we know!

WHAT IS LEFT

*"The possibility that we may annihilate not only ourselves
but the whole human future in a nuclear holocaust brings us
face to face with the mystery of our common human existence
as it forces us to confront forthrightly and in a new and
dramatic way the paradox of our finitude and our power, of
our knowing and our ultimate unknowing."* Gordon Kaufman
Harvard Divinity Bulletin, February-March 1983

We may have another year
    we may have a minute or two:
who knows when the clock will melt
    when time will shift
I mean
    into a blank space, a place
of no witnesses:
    no mother or father
    no lover or friend
I mean
    no sky alive with the voice of the wind
    no trees shining with green light
    no stone left unturned, no fragment
        of a fragment of a word to say
        love, to name innocence and mercy.

We have heard it before:
    dry sounds in the distance
    staccato notes in the symphony of war.
But we do not listen,
    do not enter the combat zone.
— A thousand wounds open
a thousand bones snap
    in the thunder-crack of battle.

Can we wake, peel the film
    from our eyes
step out of the dream
    where manna forever falls
    where quails forever flock to our dish?
We have only a moment or two
but our hands are idle, our thoughts
always turn at the same angle
    run along the same rutted tracks.

What is left to us?
To invent a new story

a new way
of being on this earth
of being together, forming
　　one luminous body
　　one sacred flesh
　　　　smooth, healthy
　　　　without remembrance of scars.

LOVING HANDS AT WORK

"Blessed are the peacemakers, they shall be called the children of God." Matthew 5:9

It may all come undone
    the patiently woven cloth
    the shawl of homespun wool.
Already now, the threads are being pulled
    life unravels at the edges
    baring the flesh, showing the scars
        the grooves dug in the wrist
        by chain and rope.

It may all come undone
    before we have time to hold
        all the parts together
    before we can gather evidence
        declare ourselves alive, say yes
        we love this sweet earth
        green-sleeved in this new spring.

It is all too quick, too soon:
    birth and death, the span
    between the poles, crossed over
    with a few steps.
And yet,
    beneath the movements, the tearing
there are loving hands at work
    mending the raveling pattern
    catching the threads
    weaving them back one by one
        into the ancient cloth.

PROGRESSION: A NATURAL HISTORY

First there was a chip of stone
    a tool of knowledge
found to be sharp, used
      to skin bear and wolf.
Then there was a village, a neighborhood
      people clustered around home fires
      sharing food, stories, a way of being
        of making sense of their lives.

Now, in between the paragraphs
there is a trough filled with a swill of words
    set out for the poor
for those hungry enough to believe
    language has explicit meaning
      is a natural truth.

What about tomorrow?
Shall survival depend
    upon the chance discovery of flint
    upon reinventing fire?
And shall anyone remember our tribe
    the name of our streets
and how it feels to be young
    to be in love, to have a child?

THE MEEK SHALL INHERIT THE EARTH

The old tools we used:
    a language of stone, words
    now flaked and worn
    thin as wafers
— nothing left
    but sounds bitter to the throat.
We still say peace, peace
    but as if spinning webs in the air
as if it were enough to speak
    when time melts down, leaving
        a residue of ashes.

Can our minds still pull
    sugar-threads of thoughts?
Can we still send messages
    of ribbons and roses?
What happened naturally
    — the slow turning of the clock
    the calming breath, the sleep
    between the white sheets of ease —
can no longer be counted
    as good measure, as common truth.
The alarm goes off, rings
    ceaselessly, louder than our wishes.
Another season is upon us:
we wake to a cave of darkness
    to a world of salt and dust.

Nothing left? A few gentle words
    passed down through the ages
        embers, containers of fire:
"The meek shall inherit the earth."

FAITH

There comes a time
    when we catch ourselves:
suddenly, a stab of recognition
suddenly, we know we are not rooted
    among immovable objects.
The foundation, the hard ground
    terra firma
no longer supports our feet.
Around us, billows of air, eddies
    of clouds, tidal waves of wind:
we are free-falling into space
    our hair streaming, our limbs
        rigid with terror
    moving rhythmically
        through a new atmosphere.

We continue to work, to pay attention
    to the life we invented, built
    like a wasp's nest, layer upon layer
    of mud and spittle to form solid walls
        caves for honey and children.
But perspectives shift:
we are traveling elsewhere
    at a speed constantly increasing
pulled away year after year
    from those clear glittering pools
    over which we danced, barely touching
        the water.
We were dragonflies, then
    childish spirits darting like answers
        in and out of the woods.
We are older now, blindly rolling
    through acres of silence, of mist;
eyes, mouth heavy with reality
    yet how light we are as we leap
        into a buoyant darkness
    where we are caught and carried
        on our way to the stars.

WAR

Some tribes, they say
    have no word for war:
they own nothing, catch fish
    with bare hands, dine
        on edible roots.

For us, war is a maggot
    a grub at the center of our speech
growing obscenely fat
    feeding on compulsions and fears.
Its bloated body curls up
    in a wound constantly enlarged;
its lips stick to all surfaces
    cling to all thoughts
    ingest all substances.

It divides itself and multiplies:
hordes of replicas crawl
    all over the map, mowing down cities
    eating through the letters of the alphabet
until no other word can be shaped
    but in its image and resemblance.
In its final stages, it is enthroned:
    a devouring idol forever feasting
        on the flesh of the world.

THE REFUGEES

They cannot be kept out:
when it comes to crossing over
    they merge with the rivers:
their sinuous bodies
    seep through the fences
      roll on the beach with the tides.
Eel-men, fish-women
    they swim dark waters
    land cold. exhausted
      on the shore.
Their scales thicken into skin
their lungs grow accustomed
    to foreign air.

When they begin to speak
    they form the sound for freedom
feel the shape of the word
    a hook piercing their tongue.
They are the inheritors
    of back-alleys, rumpled clothes
    shelves of donated food.
Only when pressed do they say
    what happens in the plazas
    after the tourists go home
    with their straw hats
      their painted pots
      their cameras.

WHAT ABOUT HOPE

Disorder, chaos, dust...
    mad twirling of people
    music of drums, of clashing notes
    the tune repeated.
Another war begins to move
    its column of ciphers
    adding guns, subtracting bread:
this is the way things are!

Forget connections
    the hands of lovers
    the touch of flesh.
The words for home, woman, child
are missing: they are bleeding
    from the mouths of dying men.

Disorder, chaos, dust...
    the condition of being human.
A mistake obviously
    to settle on this planet
this place of no return.
But, ah, what about hope
    that steady light rising
        over Bethlehem in the East?

AT THE CENTER

Hidden deeply, the seeds:
    black of loneliness
        of being singular.
No one to know
    the inner shape of the world
    the experience of germination
        of these rootlets pushing
        through the rocks, these buds
        forming themselves, a process
        no one can guess or share.

When clothes are shed
    a certain kind of truth appears
but the body is a plain text
    a simple alphabet of curves and shades.
What the hand says
    what the eye sends forth
        what the lips speak
is it enough? Are words enough
    to break through the shell of bones?

Deep within
    beyond the articulation of ecstasy
        of pain
lies a zone of utter silence:
    either a cave of darkness, a void
or, if we are willing to endure
    such beauty, such power
        a place of confluence
        a temple.

OUT OF THE LABYRINTH

"For years mothers of Plaza de Mayo have demonstrated every Thursday in Buenos Aires central square, demanding to know the fate of their missing children and other kin."
"Time" Magazine, May 16, 1983

Violence, cruelty
a line woven, darkly, within the cloth
a scream shot through the music
    in the silence between two fluted notes.
We cringe and weep:
already now we feel deep in our bones
    the beak and claws of death
hear the great wings
    immensely open over the world.

From standing figures
    — a tragic chorus
    gathering in ordinary streets —
a low moaning sound arises:
women, old and young, they lift
    banners printed with names
they hold faded photographs
    begging for news
        from the kingdom of the night.

Behind seamless walls
    in an empty archaic place
a man hangs crucified
    haloed in blood.
Stamped on his body
    the wounds of all tortured people
    the words from every language
    that speaks of tears and loss.

But he is priest and prince
    of light, of time without end.
Under his touch
the atoms of the sealing stone
    disassemble and part
and he comes clear through
    alive, full-fleshed, changing
    the density of matter
    into a new element
        supple, porous
        a weightless gauzy veil.

With him, they all return
    those who had vanished
        in the labyrinth of pain
— their names a collective:
        Lazarus
home at last from the dead.

THE INFINITE JOURNEY

Through the airways
words are shot into the room:
    murder, arson, terror in the night
    images of masked hordes
        wielding torch and knife.

We live behind enormous locks
    dream of barred windows
        protective walls and moats.
We are flesh without scale or shell
    afraid, naked, exposed.

When silence falls at last
    transparent, luminous
    a gauzy curtain wafted by the breeze
we begin to hear other sounds:
    of leaves rubbing
        one against the other
    of fluttering sparrows
        their prints on the dusty ground
            a delicate ancient script.

And deeper, beneath the crust of fear
    we discover a world as of music:
no melodies, a pulse of compressed energy
    a vibration so subtle
it cannot be recorded:
    life itself
container of heaven and earth
    of planets and constellations;
echo-chamber where all voices mingle
    of people, animals and plants;
riverbed where currents meet
    forming a single majestic flow
    moving on its infinite journey.

THE AWAKENING

What was dormant yesterday
    thoughts hardly formulated
    crawling lazily about
        like sleepy beetles
all that was half-formed
    suddenly comes into focus.
Clarity of spring!
The light beams
    into forgotten corners
        wakes our ancient roots.

It is not remembrance
    of things exhausted and past
but a surfacing, a coming through:
    green blades of knowledge
appear where yesterday
    dried stalks, skeletons of plants
rattled in the wind.

Images rise from cave depths:
    a wisdom we shared
        drawn from herb and stone
    a skill we learned together
        pulling the silk of husks
        weaving the web of dreams
            into delicate hammocks
            for lovers, for children.

It is not the work of memory:
    gone is gone.
Let the dead bury
    the bones, the broken pieces.
What comes forth now
    pushing itself into the mind:
the story of the race
    rituals and dances
    bitter-sweet words
        for sea-water, for tears.
And, newer than new
    imprinted in our blood
        since the beginning
the name above all naming
    more than light
    more than life
    impossible to say: GOD!

WE CANNOT REST

With rhythmic speed, time's shuttle flies
    from one side of the day
    to the darkening west
shaping as it goes
    the pattern and the cloth.
We fling it over our shoulders
    hold it tight around our throats.

It is colder: the wind moves
    whispers through the shriveling year.
In the backyard at dusk
    blackbirds assemble
— no song at this hour
    only screeches, metallic sounds
    hitting the winter's silence
        at different angles and levels.

Geography stretches north and south
    well past the marshes
    further than the last antarctic floe.
There are people out there
    marooned on islands of pain
    crying out louder than the birds
        in words of an alien tongue
    pleading for milk and bread.

We cannot rest: in our hands
    life thins to a single thread.
We shall draw it through the eye
    of that needle we find
        sharp as truth
    in the proverbial mess of straw.
And with pricked, trembling fingers
    we shall mend the ragged cloth
        at nightfall when the sun drowns
        in a pool of blood.

IN TIME OF WAR

Wherever I look, there is disaster:
   the hot imprint of pain
      smoking on the flesh.
Even my cats, my two innocents
   bring home tortured mice
      headless birds.
I do not wish to ask
   but questions bubble up
      grow overnight like mushrooms
         born of air and dung.

My paradise is lost
   of simple phrases
   of backyards full of children
      merry houses, games, weddings
         in the green light of summer trees.
The bread I am now kneading
   is coarse, dark-grained.
The images I now hold
   — burned in white heat
   etched with violent tools —
      can never be erased.

It is late: the year shivers
   wraps itself in woolen cloaks.
I cannot hide
   from what is cold and bleeding;
I cannot pretend
   life is but a dream
      on which to row my boat
         my precious little ark.

Where is the answer?
In what place can it be plucked
   like an extravagant useless flower
      to be laid on the bodies of the slain?
Nothing to say, no fake words
   to spray like scent
      dispelling the stench of history.
Only this:
   beyond knowledge
someone touches the sealed stone
   calls Lazarus from his stony bed.

RUN, MY SISTER!

Sorrow, sorrow, my sister
    my love!
Deep as the stone's darkest depths
    sorrow!
Rise as you must
flee as you must
    on naked bleeding feet.
Flee through smoky marshes
— the reeds bent and cracking
    as you pass.
Run, my sister! At your back
    the house burns
    the flames' red flags unroll
        from the windows
    snap in the wind.
The garden, your necklace of flowers
    unclasps, falls to powder
    in the air.
What you left, the mirrors
    the photographs, the robes you wore
        jade green, violet
        in the early mornings
    your small treasures
are now angry words the fire speaks.

Don't look! Drained of light
    the sun shrinks to a grey dot.
Run while you can
    cross rivers and mountains
    follow the blue curve of space
        to the ends of the map.
You will reach the last ridge
    peer over the rim.
Where can you go?
    In the silence
you hear the sound of your life
    clicking shut like an ivory fan
— your only witness:
    a night
        enameled with dead stars.

HOPE

"This is a very interesting time: there is no model for anything that is going on. It is a period of free fall into the future." Joseph Campbell

You begin to fall: your body
    heavy with blood and bones
drops through empty space.
Nothing to catch, no foothold
    no ledge, not a word
    on which to hang once more
        the color-flags of your life.
You descend through white silence
see the earth looming close
    an object hard and flat
    a stone of indifference.
At the last moment
    just before you hit rock-bottom
a small parachute of hope opens
    a bright corolla overhead
        held by filaments of light.
You swing free from deadly weight
float through azure currents
    in avenues of pure air.
You re-enter your daily shape
return to your voice
and land without a bruise
    on the firm ground.

RIGHT NOW

Right now, in this house we share
      — earth the name of it
      planet of no account
      in the vast ranges of the sky —
children are dying
      lambs with cracked heads
      their blood dripping on the stones.

Right now, messengers reach us
      handing out leaflets
      printed with a single word:
          death
misspelled, no longer a dusky angel
death in the shape of a vulture
      landing on broken bodies
          torn flesh.

We look elsewhere:
here the buds sliding out of their sheaths
      unroll voluptuous green leaves;
we fill the garden-room with cushions
      hang wind-bells in the trees
toss the word "death" to the flames
      over which good meat is sizzling.

Messengers are sent away
but others arrive in endless procession:
      old women, weepy-eyed, speechless
      young ones with nerves exposed.
They have crossed the sierras
they have sailed in leaky boats
they have trudged through the desert
      to say:
"Our lives have no weight:
they are made of grass, of clouds
      of stories whispered at nightfall.
We are burning fields, we are fires
      fanned by the wind."

How can we mix this knowledge
      with the bread we eat
      with the cup we drink?
Is it enough to fill these words
      these hollow flutes of bones
          with aching songs?

FOR THE FIRST TIME

For the first time, we are aware;
we hold the moment blessed
        under our breath and speech:
a drop of wine guarded
        in a translucent goblet.
One false move
        and it would shatter
the slivers to become glowing shafts
        entering the flesh
the particles to swim invisibly
        in our blood.

For the first time, we have lost the sense
        of a life to be fully lived.
We only know the hours are extended
        stretched out from dusk to dusk
their connecting thread thin
        easily cut or broken.

Shall we leave the danger zone
        roll up the carpets
store the dishes and books
        bury our hopes
                in deep iron boxes
with our names
        and the names of our children
with their toys, their sandals
        their cups?

For the first time
        we are careful of one another;
we understand
        the frail stems of flowers
        the hollowness of mouths
                empty of words
                        and screaming.

A TIME FOR PEACE

We can still make it
    gather the threads, the pieces
    each of different size and shade
    to match and sew into a pattern:
        Rose of Sharon
        wedding ring
        circles and crowns.

We can still listen:
    children at play, their voices
    mingling in the present tense
    of a time that can be extended.

Peace, we say
    looking through our pockets
to find the golden word
    the coin to buy that ease
        that place sheltered
        from bullets and bombs.

But what we seek lies elsewhere
    beyond the course of lethargic blood
    beyond the narrow dream
        of resting safe and warm.

If we adjust our lenses
    we see far in the distance
figures of marching people
    homeless, hungry, going nowhere.
Why not call them
    to our mornings of milk and bread?
The coming night will be darker
    than the heart of stones
unless we strike the match
    light the guiding candle
    say yes, there is room after all
        at the inn.

19   85

Typeset by Maria de Vinck
in twelve point Garamond
Roman Caps
eleven point Garamond
Roman and Italics
and nine point Garamond
Italics

Printed by Thomson-Shore Inc.
Dexter, Michigan

Two thousand copies constituting
the Original Edition